·FRESH FROM THE OVEN·
MUFFINS
& SMALL CAKES

HARBOUR
BOOKS

CONTENTS

MUFFINS

Cheese & Carrot Muffins 4

Cherry Muffins 6

English Muffins 8

Spicy Berry Muffins 10

SMALL CAKES

Ambrosia Cheese Squares 12

Apricot Fingers 14

Banana Honey Health Bars 16

Butterfly Cakes 18

Chocolate and Hazelnut Caramels 20

Coconut Tarts 22

Coffee Profiteroles 24

Cream Puffs 26

Crumpets 28

Crushed Fruit Meringues 30

Custard Rings 32

Doughnuts 34

Double Meringues 36

Energy Bars 38

Filo Mincemeat Bundles 40

Fritter Puffs 42

Fruity Cheesecake Slices 44

Grecian Dessert Slices 46

Lamingtons 48

Little Strawberry Shortcakes 50

Little Swiss Pancakes 52

Peaches 54

Puff Pastry Hearts 56

Sweet Potato Pecan Puffs 58

Walnut Meringues 60

Wholewheat (Wholemeal) Rock Cakes 62

CHEESE & CARROT MUFFINS

MAKES 12

1 1/4 cups (5 oz, 150 g) wholewheat (wholemeal) flour
1/2 cup (1 1/2 oz, 45 g) soy flour
1/2 teaspoon salt
2 teaspoons double-acting baking powder (1 tablespoon baking powder)
1/4 cup (1 oz, 30 g) bran, oats, barley or rice
1 onion, finely chopped
3 tablespoons polyunsaturated oil
1 carrot, grated
3 tablespoons chopped parsley
1/2 cup (4 oz, 125 g) cottage cheese
1 egg, beaten
1 cup (8 fl oz, 250 ml) soy drink or milk
3 teaspoons grated parmesan cheese or 3 tablespoons grated low-fat cheddar cheese
1 tablespoon chopped peanuts

Sift flours, salt, and baking powder into a mixing bowl. Stir in bran and make a "well" in the middle. Fry onion in oil and combine with remaining ingredients. Add to mixing bowl and stir very lightly with a fork for about fifteen stirs until combined. Don't worry if not completely mixed. Spoon into 12 greased muffin tins, sprinkle cheese and peanuts on top and bake at 375°F (190°C, Gas Mark 5) for 25 to 30 minutes until cooked.

CHERRY MUFFINS

MAKES 12

4 oz (125 g) mascarpone cheese
$1/2$ cup ($3 1/2$ oz, 100 g) demerara sugar
1 egg
2 cups (8 oz, 250 g) self-rising (raising) flour
1 cup (8 fl oz, 250 ml) milk
8 oz (250 g) fresh pitted (stoned) cherries or $13 1/2$ oz (425 g) can (tin) pitted cherries,
drained and halved
2 tablespoons demerara sugar, extra
cherries, extra
mascarpone, extra

Beat mascarpone and sugar until creamy (sugar does not dissolve so mixture will be granular). Add egg and continue beating until thoroughly mixed in.

Sift flour and lightly fold into egg mixture with cherries and milk. Do no over-mix — only until just combined.

Spoon mixture into a greased 12-cup muffin (patty) pan. Sprinkle with extra sugar. Bake in moderate oven (350°F, 180°C, Gas Mark 4) for 40 minutes or until cooked. Serve the muffins warm with extra fresh cherries and mascarpone.

ENGLISH MUFFINS

1 egg
1 1/4 cups (10 fl oz, 300 ml) tepid milk
1 oz (30 g) butter, melted and cooled
1/2 oz (15 g) fresh yeast or 1/4 oz (7 g) dried yeast
4 tablespoons tepid water
4 cups (1 lb, 500 g) all-purpose (plain) flour
1 teaspoon salt

Beat egg in a bowl and add milk and butter. Cream yeast with tepid water and set aside.

Put flour and salt in a bowl and warm in a low oven. Make a well in the middle and pour in yeast mixture, then egg-milk-butter mixture. Mix well, then knead thoroughly, adding more flour or warm water if necessary; dough should be soft and smooth. Cover bowl with a thick towel and leave in a warm place for about 1 1/2 hours or until it doubles in bulk.

Preheat oven to 450°F (230°C, Gas Mark 8). On a floured board roll dough out into a circle about 1/2 inch (1 cm) thick and cut into rounds with a biscuit cutter about 2 inches (5 cm) in diameter.

Place muffins on a floured baking tray and bake for 8 minutes, turn over and bake other side for 6 or 7 minutes until well risen.

Toast, then pull apart and butter.

SPICY BERRY MUFFINS

2 cups (8 oz, 250 g) wholewheat (wholemeal) flour
¹/₄ cup (²/₃ oz, 20 g) soy flour
2 teaspoons double-acting baking powder (1 tablespoon baking powder)
¹/₂ teaspoon ground cinnamon
¹/₂ teaspoon ground nutmeg
1 cup blueberries
1 cup small strawberries, quartered
1 egg, beaten
1 cup (8 fl oz, 250 ml) buttermilk or milk
4 tablespoons vegetable oil or melted margarine
¹/₂ cup (4 oz, 125 g) honey or raw sugar

Sift all dry ingredients into a mixing bowl. Reserve 36 blueberries, stir remainder with strawberries into dry ingredients and make a "well" in the middle. Combine all remaining ingredients, pour into middle of bowl and, using a fork, stir lightly about fifteen times until combined. Don't worry if flour is not completely mixed in. Spoon mixture into 12 greased muffin tins and top each one with 3 reserved blueberries. Bake at 375°F (190°F, Gas Mark 5) for 25 minutes or until cooked.

AMBROSIA CHEESE SQUARES

MAKES 28

3 oz (90 g) butter
1/2 cup (4 oz, 125 g) sugar
1/2 teaspoon grated orange rind
1 egg yolk
1 cup (4 oz, 125 g) all-purpose (plain) flour, sifted
1/2 cup (1 1/2 oz, 45 g) unsweetened (desiccated) coconut

AMBROSIA CHEESE TOPPING:
1 cup cottage cheese
4 oz (125 g) packaged cream cheese
1/2 cup (3 1/2 oz, 100 g) superfine (caster) sugar
1 teaspoon grated orange rind
2 eggs, separated
3 tablespoons orange juice
few drops orange food coloring
1 egg white
1/2 cup (1 1/2 oz, 45 g) unsweetened (desiccated) coconut

Cream butter, sugar, and orange rind until light. Add egg yolk and beat well, add flour and coconut. Mix to a firm dough and press into base of a greased 11 x 7 inch (28 x 18 cm) slab cake pan (tin). Bake in hot oven (425°F, 220°C, Gas Mark 7) for 10 minutes and remove. Reduce oven temperature to 325°F (160°C, Gas Mark 3). Pour topping over partly cooked base and cook, one shelf above middle, for 40 to 45 minutes until topping is set. Turn off oven and leave in oven for 30 minutes. Remove and cool thoroughly. Cut into squares, and top each with a swirl of whipped cream.

Ambrosia cheese topping: Sieve cottage cheese into a mixing bowl, add softened cream cheese, sugar, and orange rind and beat until light. Beat in egg yolks, orange juice, and food coloring. Beat egg whites until stiff and fold into cheese mixture with coconut.

APRICOT FINGERS

MAKES 20

1 1/4 cups dried apricots
6 tablespoons superfine (caster) sugar
4 oz (125 g) butter
2 cups (8 oz, 250 g) all-purpose (plain) flour, sifted
1 teaspoon double-acting baking powder (2 teaspoons baking powder)
1 egg, beaten
1 teaspoon ground cinnamon
milk

LEMON ICING:

1 cup (5 oz, 55 g) confectioners' (icing) sugar
1 tablespoon melted butter
2 teaspoons lemon juice
yellow food coloring

Soak apricots in hot water for 1 hour. Cook apricots with 3 tablespoons sugar until soft. Purée and cool. Rub butter into flour and baking powder. Add 2 tablespoons sugar and mix to a firm dough with the egg. Chill. Divide dough in half. Roll out and line a 11 x 7 inch (28 x 18 cm) greased slab cake pan (tin) with half the dough. Spread with apricot purée, sprinkle with remaining sugar and cinnamon. Cover with remaining rolled pastry, brush with milk. Bake in a hot oven (425°F, 220°C, Gas Mark 7) for 10 minutes, lower heat to 350°F (180°C, Gas Mark 4) and cook for a further 20 minutes. When cold, ice with lemon icing. Cut into fingers.

Lemon icing: Sift sugar into a bowl, add melted butter and lemon juice. Mix to a spreading consistency with boiling water. Mix in yellow food coloring.

BANANA HONEY HEALTH BARS

MAKES 20

1 cup (4 oz, 125 g) all-purpose (plain) rye flour
1 cup (4 oz, 125 g) all-purpose (plain) buckwheat flour
1 cup (6 oz, 185 g) cornmeal
1/2 cup (1 1/2 oz, 45 g) rolled oats
1 teaspoon double-acting baking powder (2 teaspoons baking powder)
1 cup (5 oz, 150 g) sun-dried bananas, sliced
1 cup (2 1/2 oz, 75 g) shredded coconut
1 cup (6 oz, 185 g) brown sugar
1 cup (3 1/3 oz, 100 g) soy compound
1 cup (5 oz, 150 g) pepitas (pumpkin seeds)
1/2 cup (4 fl oz, 125 ml) honey
1 cup (8 fl oz, 250 ml) polyunsaturated oil
1 cup (8 fl oz, 250 ml) water

Put all dry ingredients into a large mixing bowl, mix together and make a "well" in the middle. Add honey, oil, and water and mix until combined. Spread into a lined, greased shallow cake tin, 12 x 8 inches (30 x 20 cm) and bake at 375°F (180°C, Gas Mark 4) for 30 minutes. Cool on a wire cooling tray and cut into bars when cold.

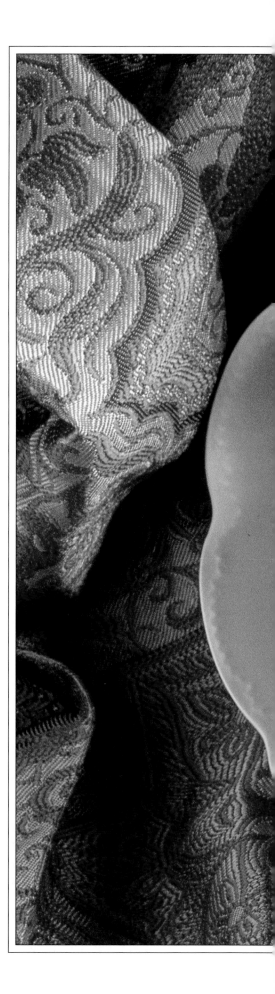

BUTTERFLY CAKES

MAKES 36

6 oz (185 g) butter
³/₄ cup (5 ¹/₂ oz, 170 g) superfine (caster) sugar
¹/₂ teaspoon vanilla extract (essence)
3 eggs
2 cups (8 oz, 250 g) self-raising flour
¹/₂ cup (4 fl oz, 125 ml) milk
jelly (jam)
whipped cream
confectioners' (icing) sugar

Preheat oven to 375–400°F, (190–200°C, Gas Mark 5–6). Butter 36 patty cake tins or line tins with paper patty cases. Cream butter, sugar, and vanilla extract until light, white and fluffy. Add beaten eggs gradually, beating well after each addition. Gently stir in sifted flour and milk. Spoon a heaped teaspoon of the mixture into each of the patty cake tins. Reduce oven temperature to moderately hot (375°F, 190°C, Gas Mark 5) and bake for approximately 15 minutes until tops have risen well and are evenly brown.

Cool on a wire rack. When cakes are cool cut a circle from the top of each using a small, sharp knife. Cut the circles in half. Place a small quantity of apricot or raspberry jelly (jam) onto each cake. Cover the jelly (jam) with 1 teaspoon of whipped cream. Replace the half circles to form butterfly wings on top of the cakes. Sprinkle the butterfly cakes lightly with sifted confectioners' sugar.

CHOCOLATE AND
HAZELNUT CARAMELS

BASE:

6 oz (175 g) all-purpose (plain) flour
pinch of salt
2 oz (60 g) light soft brown sugar or superfine (caster) sugar
4 oz (125 g) butter
1 1/2 oz (40 g) toasted hazelnuts, chopped
grated peel (rind) of 1 orange

FILLING:

4 oz (125 g) margarine
4 oz (125 g) light soft brown sugar
2 tablespoons light treacle (golden syrup)
1 small or 1/2 large can condensed milk
few drops almond extract (essence)

TOPPING:

3 oz (90 g) semi sweet (plain) chocolate
1/2 oz (15 g) butter
2 oz (60 g) white chocolate

To make the base, grease a 7 inch (18 cm) square shallow cake pan. Sift the flour and salt. Add the sugar and rub in the butter then mix in the chopped nuts and grated peel. Work into a pliable dough and press evenly into the prepared pan. Cook in a moderate oven (350°F, 180°C, Gas Mark 4) for about 25 minutes or until pale golden brown and just firm. Cool in the pan.

To make the filling, put the margarine, sugar, treacle and condensed milk into a saucepan and gently bring to a boil. Boil gently for 7–8 minutes, stirring occasionally and taking care it does not "catch". Add almond extract and beat until beginning to thicken. Pour over the base, cool and then chill thoroughly until set.

To make the topping, melt the chocolate with the butter over a pan of simmering water; stir until evenly blended. Melt the white chocolate separately.

Spread the semi-sweet chocolate over the caramel, making sure it fills the corners. Let it set slightly then drizzle the white chocolate over it. Leave until completely set, then cut into fingers or squares.

COCONUT TARTS

MAKES 30

BISCUIT PASTRY:

4 oz (125 g) butter

4 tablespoons superfine (caster) sugar

¹/₂ teaspoon vanilla extract (essence)

1 egg

2 cups (8 oz, 250 g) all-purpose (plain) flour

¹/₂ teaspoon double-acting baking powder (1 teaspoon baking powder)

raspberry jelly (jam)

COCONUT FILLING:

1 egg

¹/₂ cup (4 oz, 125 g) sugar

1 cup (3 oz, 90 g) unsweetened (dessicated) coconut

Beat butter, sugar, and vanilla until light. Add egg and beat well. Sift flour and baking powder and mix into butter mixture. Knead lightly on a floured board, roll out to ¹/₄ inch (5 mm) thick and cut into rounds to fit small tart pans (tins). Place a scant half teaspoon of jelly in base of each tart, top with a generous teaspoon of coconut filling, spreading it over jelly (jam). Bake in a hot oven (425°F, 220°C, Gas Mark 7) for 15 minutes. Remove from tart tins and cool on a wire rack.

Coconut filling: Beat egg lightly and mix in sugar and coconut until blended.

COFFEE PROFITEROLES

MAKES 16

2 1/2 oz (65 g) all-purpose (plain) flour
pinch of salt
2 oz (60 g) butter
2/3 cup (5 fl oz, 150 ml) water
2 eggs, beaten

PRALINE CREAM:

3 oz (90 g) unblanched almonds
3 oz (90 g) superfine (caster) sugar
1 1/4 cups (10 fl oz, 300 ml) heavy (double) cream

COFFEE GLACÉ ICING:

6 oz (175 g) confectioners' (icing) sugar, sifted
2–3 teaspoons coffee extract (essence) or very strong black coffee

Mix salt into flour. Put butter and water into a saucepan and gently bring to a boil. Add flour all at once and mix with a wooden spoon until it forms a ball and leaves sides of pan clean.

Remove from heat and spread paste out evenly over base of pan. Leave to cool for about 10 minutes, then beat eggs vigorously into the paste, a little at a time, until smooth and glossy (the paste may not need all of the egg). Put into a piping bag fitted with a 3/4 inch (2 cm) plain vegetable nozzle and pipe round balls about one and a half times the size of a walnut, well apart, onto well-greased baking trays. Cook in a hot oven (425°F, 220°C, Gas Mark 7) for 25 to 30 minutes or until well puffed up, golden brown and firm to the touch. Take out of oven and pierce each one close to the base with a skewer to let steam escape. Put into turned-off oven for 2 to 3 minutes to dry out. Cool on a wire rack.

Praline cream: Put almonds and sugar into a heavy-based pan and heat gently until sugar melts. Cook slowly until golden brown, then turn quickly onto an oiled baking tray or piece of parchment (baking paper). Leave until cold and set, then crush with a rolling pin. Whip cream and fold in the praline.

Put into a piping bag with a 1/4 inch (5 mm) plain piping nozzle, insert the nozzle in the holes in bases of buns and pipe in cream filling.

Coffee glacé icing: Put confectioners' sugar in a bowl and gradually work in coffee extract until thick (add a little hot water if necessary). Carefully dip top of each bun in icing so it is well covered, then leave to set on a wire rack.

CREAM PUFFS & ECLAIRS

CHOUX PASTRY:

1 1/4 cups (10 fl oz, 310 ml) water
4 oz (125 g) butter
1/2 tablespoon sugar
1 1/4 cups (5 oz, 250 g) all-purpose (plain) flour
4 eggs

FILLING:

20 fl oz (500 ml) cream
4 tablespoons confectioners' (icing) sugar

Put the water, butter and sugar in a saucepan over medium heat. Sieve the flour onto a piece of paper. When the water is boiling and butter dissolved, quickly pour the flour into the saucepan, stirring rapidly with a wooden spoon.

Continue until mixture forms a soft ball and leaves the sides of the saucepan. Remove from heat, allow to cool for 2 minutes. Beat eggs slightly, add to the mixture a quarter at a time and beat well until a satin-like sheen develops on the mixture.

Preheat oven to 400–450°F (200–230°C, Gas Mark 6–8). Lightly grease a baking sheet (oven tray). Place a 1/2 inch (1 cm) plain piping (icing) tube into a forcing bag. Put the choux pastry into the bag.

For cream puffs, pipe small pieces onto the baking sheet about the size of a large walnut at least 3 inches (7 cm) apart. For éclairs, pipe desired lengths of mixture.

Liberally sprinkle the puffs or éclairs and the baking sheet with water. Cover with an inverted roasting pan to keep in the steam.

Bake for 20 to 25 minutes in the hot oven, then reduce temperature to moderate (350–375°F, 180–190°C, Gas Mark 4–5) and bake for a further 10 minutes. The puffs or éclairs should be crisp, light and evenly golden. Remove from baking sheet to a wire cooling tray. When cool, cut open across the middle.

To fill, whip the cream, pipe into cream puffs or éclairs and sprinkle heavily with confectioners' sugar.

CRUMPETS

4 cups (1 lb, 500 g) all purpose (plain) flour
¹/₂ oz (15 g) fresh yeast or ¹/₄ oz (7 g) dried yeast
2 ¹/₂ oz (75 g) powdered milk
2 teaspoons salt
2 ³/₄ cups (22 fl oz, 700 ml) tepid water
1 teaspoon baking soda (bicarbonate of soda) mixed with 4 tablespoons tepid water

Put flour in a large oven-proof bowl and warm in a low oven.

Dissolve yeast in 2 tablespoons of tepid water. Add powdered milk and salt to flour, making a well in the middle. Add yeast mixture, remaining water, and beat until very smooth and elastic — about 5 minutes by hand, less time in a food processor.

Cover bowl with plastic wrap (film) and leave in a warm place for about 1¹/₂ hours or until batter doubles in bulk and surface is bubbly.

Add baking soda mixture and beat well. Leave dough to stand for 15 minutes.

Lightly grease a griddle or electric frying pan and four crumpet or egg rings. Heat griddle until very hot and place rings on it. With a large spoon, ladle batter into rings, filling to about half their depth (it will be hard to pour as it is very rubbery). They should rise immediately and holes start to appear on surface. If no holes appear, add a little more water to batter.

As soon as surface of crumpets start to look dry — 3 to 4 minutes — turn crumpets over and cook on other side for 30 seconds. Set aside and make the rest of the crumpets.

Toast lightly and spread with butter.

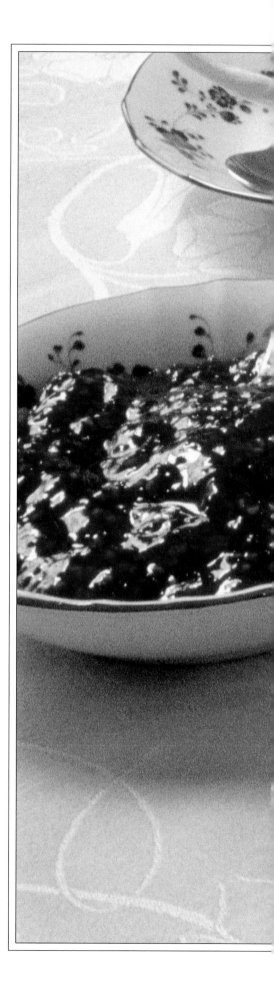

CRUSHED FRUIT MERINGUES

4 egg whites
1 good cup (8 oz, 250 g) superfine (caster) sugar
^{1}/4 teaspoon cream of tartar
few drops vanilla extract (essence)
10 fl oz (300 ml) whipped cream
^{1}/2 cup crushed fruit

Whisk egg whites until stiff. Gradually add sugar a teaspoon at a time, beating continuously. Fold in cream of tartar, then vanilla. Line greased baking trays with greased, waxed (greaseproof) paper. Put teaspoons of meringue mix on prepared trays or use a forcing bag.

Put in cool oven (225°F, 110°C, Gas Mark ^{1}/4) to dry out for 1 to 2 hours. When cool, join together with whipped cream mixed with crushed fruit.

CUSTARD RINGS

CHOUX PASTRY:

1 1/4 cups (10 fl oz, 310 ml) water

4 oz (125 g) butter

1/2 tablespoon sugar

1 1/4 cups (5 oz, 250 g) all-purpose (plain) flour

4 eggs

CUSTARD FILLING:

20 fl oz (600 ml) milk

2 tablespoons sugar

1/2 oz (15 g) butter

4 tablespoons cornstarch (cornflour)

3 drops vanilla extract (essence)

3 drops yellow coloring

2 large eggs

DECORATION:

4 oz (125 g) chocolate

2 oz (60 g) toasted flaked almonds

Choux Pastry: Put the water, butter and sugar in a saucepan over medium heat. Sieve the flour onto a piece of paper. When the water is boiling and butter dissolved, quickly pour the flour into the saucepan, stirring rapidly with a wooden spoon. Continue until mixture forms a soft ball and leaves the sides of the saucepan. Remove from heat, allow to cool for 2 minutes. Beat eggs slightly, add to mixture a quarter at a time and beat well until a satin-like sheen develops.

Pastry rings: Preheat oven to 400°F (200–230°C, Gas Mark 6–8). Grease a baking sheet (oven tray). Take a 2 inch (5 cm) pastry cutter, dip the edge in flour, then mark circles on sheet 2 inches (5 cm) apart. Pipe the pastry with a 1/2 inch (1 cm) plain tube in a forcing bag, piping around the edge of the marked ring on the sheet. Sprinkle with water. Bake for 20 minutes in the hot oven then reduce heat to moderate (350–375°F, 180–190°C, Gas Mark 4–5) for 5 minutes. The rings should be crisp, light and golden. Remove from baking sheet to a wire cooling tray.

Custard filling: Put 15 fl oz (450 ml) milk, sugar and butter in a saucepan and bring to a boil. Blend cornstarch with remaining milk, vanilla extract and yellow coloring. When milk has boiled lower heat, pour in blended cornstarch and stir with a whisk or wooden spoon until thickened and smooth. Remove from heat, cool for 2 minutes. Pour lightly beaten egg into custard and mix till smooth.

To finish Custard Rings: Slice choux pastry rings through middle. Pipe custard on top of base with a 1/2 inch (1 cm) tube. Melt chocolate in a heatproof bowl or in top of double boiler over simmering water, dip smooth side of top of ring into the melted chocolate, place on top of base and sprinkle with toasted almonds.

DOUGHNUTS

MAKES 12

2 cups (8 oz, 250 g) all-purpose (plain) flour
1/4 teaspoon baking soda (bicarbonate of soda)
1/2 teaspoon cream of tartar
1/4 teaspoon ground nutmeg
1/2 teaspoon ground cinnamon
1/4 cup (2 oz, 60 g) superfine (caster) sugar
1 egg
1/2 cup (4 fl oz, 125 ml) sour milk
1 tablespoon melted butter
oil for frying
cinnamon sugar for coating

Sift dry ingredients into a bowl. Beat egg lightly and add with sour milk and melted butter to flour. Mix to a soft dough. Turn onto a floured board and knead lightly. Roll out till about 1/4 inch (5 mm) thick and cut into rings with a floured doughnut cutter or a large and a very small cookie (biscuit) cutter.

Fry 3 or 4 at a time in deep, hot oil for 3 to 4 minutes, turning them to brown evenly. Drain on absorbent paper and coat with cinnamon sugar (ie superfine sugar mixed with ground cinnamon).

Note: To sour milk, add 2 teaspoons vinegar or lemon juice to 1/2 cup fresh milk. Leave at room temperature for 10 to 15 minutes if milk is icy cold.

DOUBLE MERINGUES

2 egg whites
4 oz (125 g) superfine (caster) sugar

FILLING:

1 cup (8 fl oz, 250 ml) heavy (double) cream
1 tablespoon liqueur, rum or brandy (optional)
2 oz (60 g) semi-sweet (plain) chocolate

Line two or three baking trays with parchment (baking paper).

Put the egg whites in a grease-free bowl and whisk until very stiff and dry, standing in peaks.

Whisk in sugar a tablespoon at a time, making sure meringue is stiff again before adding further sugar.

Spoon meringue mix into even heaps, shaping them with two dessertspoons; or use a large piping bag with a large star or plain vegetable nozzle.

Cook in a very cool oven (225°F, 110°C, Gas Mark 1/4) for 1 1/2 to 2 hours until crisp and dry and they peel easily off the paper. Leave to cool on the baking sheets. Unfilled, they will keep in an airtight container for up to two weeks.

Filling: Whip cream with liqueur, until stiff, then put in a piping bag with a large star vegetable nozzle. Pipe a whirl onto base of one meringue and sandwich together with another. Melt chocolate in a bowl over a pan of gently simmering water, stir until smooth then drizzle chocolate over meringues.

Brown sugar meringues: Replace half superfine sugar with light soft brown sugar and sift together twice before you begin. The insides will be more gooey than normal meringues and may tend to stick to the paper a little.

ENERGY BARS

MAKES 16

3 cups (12 oz, 375 g) wholewheat (wholemeal) flour
1/4 cup (2/3 oz, 20 g) soy flour
1/2 cup (2 1/2 oz, 75 g) soy grits (coarsely ground)
1 cup (3 1/2 oz, 100 g) dried soy compound
1 teaspoon double-acting baking powder (2 teaspoons baking powder)
1 cup (6 oz, 185 g) brown sugar
1 1/2 cups (6 oz, 185 g) seedless raisins
1 cup pepitas (pumpkin seeds) or sunflower kernels
1/4 cup (3 oz, 90 g) molasses or treacle
3/4 cup (6 fl oz, 185 ml) polyunsaturated oil
1 cup (8 fl oz, 250 ml) water

Put all dry ingredients in a large mixing bowl and make a "well" in the middle.
Add remaining ingredients and mix well to combine. Pour mixture into a lined
and greased shallow tin 12 x 8 inch (30 x 20 cm) and bake at 350°F (180°C,
Gas Mark 4) for 30 to 40 minutes, until cooked. Cool in tin then cut into bars.
Store in an airtight container.

FILO MINCEMEAT BUNDLES

MAKES 12

6 oz (175 g) mincemeat
grated peel (rind) of 1 orange
2 tablespoons brandy or rum
2 dessert apples, peeled, cored and coarsely grated
2 level tablespoons chopped blanched almonds or hazelnuts
12 sheets filo pastry, thawed if frozen
about 3 oz (90 g) butter, melted
confectioners' (icing) sugar, for dredging

These bundles are a mixture of grated apple, orange peel, brandy and mincemeat encased in sheets of filo pastry pinched together at the top and dredged with confectioners' sugar.

Put the mincemeat into a bowl and mix in the orange peel and brandy. Add the apple and the nuts and mix well.

Cut each sheet of pastry in half to give two squares. Put one square on a flat surface and brush with melted butter. Place another square on top in a diamond position, about a 45° angle. Its corners should be midway between the corners of the first square. Brush again with melted butter.

Place a heaped teaspoon of the mincemeat mixture in the middle of the pastry and carefully gather up the edges and pinch tightly together, allowing the tips of the pastry to fall over. Stand on greased baking sheets and carefully brush all over withe melted butter. Repeat with the rest of the pastry.

Cook in a moderately hot oven (375°F, 190°C, Gas Mark 5) for about 20 minutes or until a light golden brown and the pastry is cooked through. Remove to a wire rack and dredge with sifted confectioners' sugar. Leave until cold, and serve as they are or with whipped cream.

FRITTER PUFFS

MAKES 24

2 large eggs
¹/₂ cup (4 oz, 120 g) superfine (caster) sugar
2 tablespoons cold water
¹/₄ cup (2 oz, 60 ml) virgin olive oil
finely grated peel (rind) and juice of ¹/₂ lemon
1¹/₂ cups (6 oz, 185 g) all-purpose (plain) flour
³/₄ teaspoon double-acting baking powder (1 ¹/₂ teaspoons baking powder)
2 cups (16 fl oz, 500 ml) olive or vegetable oil
superfine (caster) sugar or confectioners' (icing) sugar

In a mixing bowl whisk the eggs, sugar, and water together until light. Add the oil and lemon and mix in well. Sift in the flour and baking powder and stir in. Cover the bowl and set aside for 30 minutes.

Heat oil in a deep pan until almost smoking, then reduce heat slightly. Drop tablespoonfuls of the batter into the hot oil, no more than 5 at a time, and cook until puffed and golden brown. Turn once only, cook the other side and then remove with a slotted spoon. Drain on a rack covered with paper towels. Dust thickly with sugar.

Tip: When cold, the puffs can be slit open at one side and filled with sweetened, whipped cream.

FRUITY CHEESECAKE SLICES

6 oz (175 g) all-purpose (plain) flour
pinch of salt
3 oz (90 g) superfine (caster) sugar
3 oz (90 g) butter, softened
3 egg yolks

FILLING:

8 oz (250 g) full fat soft cream cheese
4 egg yolks
2 oz (60 g) butter, melted
8 oz (250 g) superfine (caster) or light soft brown sugar
grated peel (rind) of 1 orange or lemon
1 tablespoon orange flower water

TOPPING:

6 oz (175 g) confectioners' (icing) sugar, sifted
few pieces glacé pineapple, glacé cherries and other glacé fruits
few pieces angelica, cut into narrow strips

Pâte sucrée: Sift flour and salt onto a work surface, make a well in the middle and add sugar, butter, and egg yolks. Using fingertips, pinch and work ingredients together then gradually work in flour to make a smooth pliable dough. Wrap in plastic (cling) wrap or foil and chill for an hour.

Roll out the pastry carefully. Lightly grease a rectangular pan (tin) 11 x 7 x 1 1/2 inches (28 x 18 x 4 cm) and line it with pastry. Trim and crimp edges, spoon in filling, leveling the top.

Cook in a moderate oven (350°F, 180°C, Gas Mark 4) for about 1 hour or until quite firm. Leave in pan to cool. When cold cut into slices and decorate with topping.

Filling: Beat cheese until smooth, then beat in egg yolks, butter, sugar, fruit peel, and orange flower water. Spoon into pan and level the top.

Topping: Decorate slices with pieces of glacé fruit and angelica and sprinkle with confectioners' sugar.

GRECIAN DESSERT SLICES

MAKES 8

8 oz (250 g) butter or margarine, softened
1 cup (8 oz, 250 g) superfine (caster) sugar
1 teaspoon vanilla extract (essence)
4 eggs, separated
1 1/2 cups (6 oz, 185 g) self-rising (raising) flour
2 teaspoons mixed spices
2 teaspoons grated lemon rind
1 1/2 cups (8 oz, 250 g) fine farina (semolina)

SYRUP:

1/2 cup (4 oz, 125 g) sugar
1/2 cup (5 oz, 155 g) honey
1 cup (8 fl oz, 250 ml) water
1 tablespoon lemon juice
whole cloves, for decoration

Preheat oven to 350°F (180°C, Gas Mark 4). Line and grease a 9 inch (23 cm) slab pan (tin). Beat butter, sugar, and vanilla until creamy; add egg yolks and beat well. Sift flour with spices; add lemon rind and farina, and mix well.

Whisk egg whites well (do not beat stiffly). Into butter-egg mixture, fold alternate batches of dry ingredients and beaten egg whites, about a third of each at a time. Spoon mixture into pan, and bake for 35 to 40 minutes.

Syrup: Combine ingredients, bring slowly to a boil, simmer 7 to 8 minutes.

Slowly spoon the cooled syrup over cooked cake so that it is absorbed. Cut and cool in pan. Decorate with cloves.

LAMINGTONS

4 oz (125 g) butter or margarine, softened
³/4 cup (6 oz, 185 g) superfine caster sugar
1 teaspoon vanilla extract (essence)
2 eggs
¹/2 cup (4 fl oz, 125 ml) milk
2 cups (8 oz, 250 g) self-raising flour
¹/4 teaspoon salt

ICING:

2 cups (12 oz) confectioners' (icing) sugar
2 tablespoons cocoa
1 oz (30 g) butter or margarine
3–4 tablespoons boiling milk or water
2²/3 cups (8 oz, 250 g) shredded (desiccated) coconut

Preheat oven to 350°F (180°C, Gas Mark 4). Thoroughly grease a 8–9 inch (20–23 cm) slab tin.

Beat the butter, sugar, and vanilla extract until light and fluffy. Add the eggs one at a time, beating well after each addition. Beat as much of the milk into the mixture as possible without it beginning to "curdle", then lightly fold in the sifted flour and salt and the remaining milk. Spoon into the tin.

Bake for 35 to 40 minutes. Let stand for 2 to 3 minutes, then turn out onto a cake rack. When cold, cut into 16 squares and set aside for several hours before icing.

Icing: Sift icing sugar and cocoa into a bowl. Combine butter and boiling milk, and pour into the icing sugar mixture to form a creamy consistency. Stand the bowl over a container of hot water to keep the icing from setting too quickly.

Using a long-pronged fork for holding each cake square, dip each piece into the chocolate icing and twist to coat all sides. Put the shredded coconut on a flat plate, and toss each iced square in it to coat thoroughly. Lift onto a cake rack to set; store in an airtight container until ready for use.

Note: You can use a packet butter cake if desired.

LITTLE STRAWBERRY SHORTCAKES

MAKES 8

8 oz (250 g) self-rising (raising) flour
1/2 level teaspoon double-acting baking powder (1 level teaspoon baking powder)
pinch of salt
3 oz (90 g) butter
2 oz (60 g) superfine (caster) sugar
1 egg, beaten
1–3 tablespoons milk

FILLING:

3/4–1 lb (350–450 g) fresh strawberries
3 level tablespoons superfine (caster) sugar
1 1/4 cups (10 fl oz, 300 ml) heavy (double) cream
few drops of vanilla extract (essence) or 1 tablespoon rum

Sift flour, baking powder, and salt into a bowl and rub in butter until mixture resembles fine breadcrumbs. Stir in sugar. Add egg and sufficient milk to make a pliable dough. Knead lightly and divide dough into eight even-sized pieces.

Roll out pieces of dough into rounds of 3 inches (7 1/2 cm) diameter, or stamp out into rounds with a cutter.

Put on a lightly greased baking tray, cook in a moderately hot oven (375°F, 190°C, Gas Mark 5) for about 15 minutes or until well risen and light golden brown. Cool on wire rack.

Filling: Keep 8 large strawberries for decoration and slice remainder into a bowl. Mix in sugar. Whip cream with vanilla or rum and fold about half of it through the strawberries.

Split shortcakes in half horizontally and fill with strawberry cream mixture. Put remaining whipped cream in a piping bag fitted with large star vegetable nozzle and pipe a large whirl of cream on each shortcake. Top each with strawberries. Chill until ready to serve.

LITTLE SWISS PANCAKES

MAKES 8

FILLING:

8 oz (250 g) packet cream cheese
2 teaspoons superfine (caster) sugar
4 drops vanilla extract (essence)
10 fl oz (300 ml) heavy (double) cream
8 oz (250 g) black cherry jelly (jam)

PANCAKES:

1 cup (4 oz, 125 g) self-raising flour
¹/₄ teaspoon bicarbonate of soda
¹/₄ teaspoon cream of tartar
1 tablespoon superfine (caster) sugar
1 large egg
5 fl oz (150 ml) milk
margarine for greasing

Sift flour, sugar, bicarbonate of soda and cream of tartar into a mixing bowl. Make a well in the middle, add egg and milk gradually and beat with a wooden spoon until smooth.

Lightly grease a heavy-based frying pan with margarine and place over a medium heat. When hot, drop one metal tablespoon of batter onto surface to make a neat round. Continue until surface is covered with pancakes but allow space to turn. When the tops begin to bubble and the undersides are slightly golden, turn over with a palette knife and cook until the other sides are golden.

Cool the drop scones on a wire rack between clean cloths.

Put cream cheese in a mixing bowl, add superfine sugar, vanilla extract and 3 tablespoons cream and beat well until smooth.

Spread the cream cheese mixture over 8 pancakes and top with the remaining 8 pancakes.

Put the sandwiched pancakes on a broiler (grill) pan and carefully put a teaspoon of cream on top of each one. Put under a very hot broiler for ¹/₂ to 1 minute.

Put 1 or 2 teaspoons black cherry jelly on top of each pancake and serve immediately with a bowl of remaining cream, whipped, and extra black cherry jelly.

PEACHES

4 oz (125 g) butter or margarine, softened
¹/₂ cup (4 oz, 125 g) sugar
3 eggs
¹/₂ cup (4 fl oz, 125 ml) milk
orange food coloring
2 cups (8 oz, 250 g) self-rising (raising) flour

DECORATION:

strawberry jelly (jam)

MOCK CREAM FILLING — BOILED:

1 ¹/₄ cups (10 fl oz, 300 ml) milk
2 tablespoons cornstarch (cornflour)
2 oz (60 g) butter or margarine
1 teaspoon vanilla extract (essence)
2 tablespoons confectioners' (icing) sugar
strawberry and orange jello (gelatin) crystals
boiling water

Preheat oven to 400°F (200°C, Gas Mark 6). Place small-cavity gem irons in oven to heat. Cream butter and sugar well. Add eggs one at a time, beating well after each addition; add milk with a little food coloring and beat thoroughly. Fold sifted flour through lightly.

Grease heated gem irons and two-thirds fill cavities with cake mixture. Bake for 14 to 16 minutes. Turn onto cake racks to cool.

Decoration: Scoop out a little mixture from top of each cake; fill with jelly. Join two cakes together with Mock Cream, chill well.

Dissolve ¹/₄ cup (1 ¹/₂ oz, 45 g) of jello crystals in ¹/₂ cup (4 fl oz, 125 ml) boiling water; cool until thickens, then brush over cakes.

Toss cakes lightly in combined strawberry and orange jello crystals to coat. Chill to set.

Mock Cream: Blend 3 tablespoons of milk with cornstarch.

Heat remaining milk in saucepan, until boiling. Gradually add blended cornstarch and stir briskly until smooth. Lower heat and simmer for 1 to 2 minutes, then take off heat and cool.

Beat butter, vanilla, and confectioners' sugar until creamy. Gradually add milk mixture, beating well between each addition.

PUFF PASTRY HEARTS

8 oz (250 g) puff pastry, thawed if frozen
superfine (caster) sugar

FILLING:

8 fl oz (250 ml) heavy (double) cream
1 1/2 teaspoons confectioners' (icing) sugar, sifted
few drops vanilla or almond extract (essence) or 1 tablespoon rum or other liqueur
little jelly (jam), of your choice

Lightly grease two or three baking trays. Roll out pastry thinly on lightly floured surface and trim to rectangle of about 12 x 10 inches (30 x 25 cm). Dredge with sugar. Fold long sides halfway to middle of pastry and again dredge with sugar. Fold folded sides right to middle of pastry and again dredge with sugar; fold in half lengthwise to hide other folds. Press together lightly.

Cut through fold into 12 slices and place on baking trays with the cut sides downwards and well apart. Open tip of each a little and flatten slightly with a round-bladed knife.

Dredge with a little more sugar and cook in a hot oven (425°F, 220°C, Gas Mark 7) for 7 to 10 minutes until golden brown. Turn over carefully and continue to cook for a further 4 to 5 minutes until golden brown. Cool on wire rack. When cold, can be stored in airtight container until needed. Can be served plain if desired.

Filling: Whip cream until stiff and fold in confectioners' sugar and extract or liqueur. Spread six pastries with a thin layer of jelly and cover liberally with whipped cream. Top with a second pastry. Can be chilled until required.

Spicy puff pastry hearts: Mix 1 teaspoon ground cinnamon or mixed spice with sugar before dredging the pastry.

SWEET POTATO PECAN PUFFS

MAKES 8

2 cups (8 oz, 250 g) all-purpose (plain) flour
1 1/4 teaspoons double-acting baking powder (2 1/2 teaspoons baking powder)
1/2 teaspoon baking soda (bicarbonate of soda)
1/2 teaspoon salt
1/4 cup (2 fl oz, 60 ml) vegetable oil
3/4 cup (6 fl oz, 175 ml) buttermilk or 3/4 cup (6 fl oz, 175 ml) milk plus
1 teaspoon lemon juice
1 cup (8 oz, 250 g) mashed cooked sweet potatoes or yams (about 3/4 lb (350 g) raw)
1/2 teaspoon ground ginger
1/4 teaspoon ground allspice
1/4 cup (1 oz, 30 g) chopped pecans
1 tablespoon molasses
1 tablespoon sugar

Preheat oven to 450°F (230°C, Gas Mark 8). Thoroughly mix the flour, baking powder, baking soda, and salt. Blend the remaining ingredients in another bowl and add to the flour mixture all at once. Stir only until evenly combined.

With a tablespoon, spoon the dough onto a lightly oiled baking sheet (oven tray). Uncooked puffs should be about 2 inches (5 cm) in diameter, spaced at least 1 inch (2.5 cm) apart.

Bake for about 15 minutes or until puffed and lightly browned.

WALNUT MERINGUES

2 egg whites
5 oz (150 g) confectioners' (icing) sugar, sifted
1 1/2 oz (40 g) walnuts, pecans, almonds, or filberts (hazelnuts), toasted and chopped
1 cup (8 fl oz, 250 g) heavy (double) cream
1 tablespoon coffee extract (essence) or milk
9–10 cape gooseberries or cumquats
2–3 Chinese gooseberries (kiwi fruits), peeled

Line two baking trays with parchment (baking paper)

Put egg whites and sugar into heatproof bowl and place over saucepan of gently simmering water. Whisk mixture until it stands in stiff peaks.

Remove bowl from heat and continue to whisk for a minute or so, then beat in nuts. Spoon mixture into a piping bag with largest plain vegetable nozzle and onto baking trays pipe rounds about 2 1/2–3 inches (7–7 1/2 cm) diameter.

Cook in cool oven (300°F, 150°C, Gas Mark 2) for about 30 minutes or until pale cream and will lift off paper easily. Cool on paper. When cold, will keep in airtight container for up to two weeks.

Whip cream with coffee extract or milk until stiff enough to pipe, but not over stiff. Put into piping bag with large star vegetable nozzle and pipe a large whirl on top of each meringue. Decorate with cape gooseberries or cumquats and halved slices of peeled Chinese gooseberries. Chill until required.

WHOLEWHEAT (WHOLEMEAL) ROCK CAKES

MAKES 20

1 cup (4 oz, 125 g) self-rising (raising) flour
1 cup (5 oz, 155 g) wholewheat (wholemeal) self-rising (raising) flour
¹/₂ teaspoon mixed spice
¹/₄ teaspoon ground nutmeg
¹/₂ cup (4 oz, 125 g) raw sugar
3 oz (90 g) butter
¹/₂ cup (3 ¹/₂ oz, 100 g) dried mixed fruit
1 egg
¹/₄ cup (2 fl oz, 60 ml) milk

Sift flours and spices into a mixing bowl, adding any grist left in sifter. Blend in sugar. Rub butter into flour mixture until crumbly. Stir in dried fruit. Beat egg and add with milk. Mix quickly to a soft dough using a round-bladed knife.

Place rough tablespoons of the dough onto a greased baking tray and bake in a hot oven (425°F, 220°C, Gas Mark 7) for 12 to 15 minutes until golden brown. Serve warm or cold with butter.

Published by Harbour Books
PO Box 48, Millers Point NSW 2000, Australia

First published in 1996
Reprinted 1997

© Copyright: Harbour Books 1996
© Copyright design: Harbour Books 1996

ISBN 1 86302 508 1